LET'S go, JESUS,

written by Karen Speerstra
illustrated by Fred Stout

Concordia

Publishing House
St. Louis

Let's Go, Jesus was inspired by and is dedicated to the two "big movers" in my life—Joel, 11, and Nathan, 8.

Concordia Publishing House, St. Louis, Missouri
Copyright © 1977 Concordia Publishing House
MANUFACTURED IN THE UNITED STATES OF AMERICA

Library of Congress Cataloging in Publication Data

Speerstra, Karen.
    Let's go, Jesus.

    SUMMARY: Conversation-prayers with Jesus which deal with such common events of a child's life as going to the hospital, planting a garden, taking piano lessons, and flying a kite.
    1. Children—Prayer-books and devotions—English.
[1. Prayer books and devotions] I. Stout, Fred.
II. Title.

BV4870.S66   242'.6'2   77-24030
ISBN 0-570-03468-X

Introduction to adults:

In His hillside sermons, Jesus said, "Let the children come to Me." He requested their company. Surely He must have enjoyed their inquisitive fingers clutching at His sleeves and their busy toes bumping against His sandals. He must have been intrigued by their vivid imaginations and agile young minds.

When He said, "Come," my guess is that the children looked at each other for a brief second and then replied, "Let's go."

The relationship those children had with Jesus was tactile and physically real.

Blessed are today's children who have neither seen nor touched Him but are still willing to say, "Let's go."

This book attempts to capture the conversations that might take place as an elementary-aged child moves about his world with Jesus at his side. *Let's Go, Jesus* requests Christ's company in a time that says "now" to a child.

It is my wish that you will use this book in a variety of ways, not the least of which is just reading it for the joy of hearing the sounds of the words.

These short conversational-action prayers or "reflections" also might prove to be discussion starters dealing with these theological concepts:

Grace ....Let's go the circus
Faith ....Let's go to the hospital
                  Let's plant our garden
Eternity and
  time ....Let's go to church
Love ....Let's go to Grandma's and
                      Grandpa's
                  Let's go build a birdhouse
                  Let's go to the dentist
Creation ....Let's go the the planetarium
                  Let's go camping
Freedom ....Let's play the piano
Sin and
  forgiveness ....Let's go fly a kite
Baptism ....Let's go beachcombing
Stewardship ......Let's go hunt for treasure
Redemption ......Let's go skating
God's
  omniscience ...Let's go make a "God's Eye"
Prayer ....Let's go play chess
Christ's kingship .Let's go to the supermarket
Christian
  responsibility ...Let's go feed the fish
                  Let's go to the zoo
Resurrection ......Let's go see if my
                      caterpillar has hatched
Advent ....Let's go to my friend's
                      birthday party
God's presence ...Let's go on our vacation

It is also my hope that in reading this book children will come away from it with a more concrete picture of Jesus as a historical person who at one time was a very real little boy.

The Biblical passages in this book are from THE HOLY BIBLE FOR CHILDREN, © 1977 Concordia Publishing House.

Karen Speerstra

Introduction to children:

You know how you sprint through your days and bounce up to bedtime only to discover that even when your body tries to be still your brain keeps right on moving.

It's hard to be still. Chances are that when Jesus was a boy He wasn't too still, either.

After He grew up and began teaching people about our Father's love, sometimes children came along with their parents to hear Him speak. His disciples were concerned that the children would bother Him. But He set them straight. He said, "Let the children come to Me."

Jesus invited *you.*

Pretend that you say to Jesus, "O.K., Jesus. You want me to come to You, and I want You to be with me. So, let's move together."

If you say this to Jesus, He's going to be with you. All day. Everyday. No matter what you are doing or who you are with, He's there.

What will you and Jesus talk about?

Karen Speerstra

Back when You were on earth the Romans had circuses, too. Did You ever go? Did You see any elephants? Our circuses don't have gladiators that kill anybody or lions that eat people—unless the lions get out of their cages.

A man named Al Ringling got our circuses started. He used to balance an old-fashioned plow on his chin, and people bought tickets to see him do it. Then he hired more people and got wagons to haul animals in, and he put up big tents. Pretty soon he called his big tent the "big top."

Circuses are exciting. I think the music makes my heart speed up. Just smell that popcorn!

Let's go to
the circus, Jesus.

Of all the things in the circus, I like the clowns best of all. When You were on earth I'm sure You could make people laugh and feel good inside.

My mom said once clowns are the glue that holds the circus together. You're kind of like glue, too, aren't You, Jesus? You make people want to stick together.

Learning about You is fun. Being with You is as much fun as being at the circus. You make me feel happy. I like being with You!

Give me again the joy of being saved by You.

Psalm 51:12

I have to have my tonsils taken out. Mom and Dad say it's going to hurt, but the hurt won't last long. Since You know all about what it feels like to hurt, I'd just as soon You were right there next to me.

It's not that hospitals scare me so much. I know what TV hospitals are like, and I visited our hospital with my class from school. It's just that, besides Dr. Smith, I don't know anybody there. If You come along, I'll at least know Somebody else. And You have a way of not getting in the way, so they won't make You leave after visiting hours.

Hospitals smell kind of funny. Everything's so white. It bothers me to be so clean.

Will You sort of help my doctor tomorrow

morning so he does a good job? When I go to sleep under those bright surgery lights, I'll know You're watching.

You used to heal people just by touching them, didn't You? You were some doctor! You must have been busy. But You were never too busy to spend time with kids. That's what I like about You. Some grownups—even Dr. Smith sometimes—act as if we aren't really there. They sort of talk through us and hurry around us. But not You. You really care. That's why I want You to come along with me to the hospital.

Throw all your cares and worries on God because He cares for you.

1 Peter 5:7

Let's go to the hospital, Jesus

Dad says I can have a special spot in our big garden to grow anything I want to grow.

Seeds must be the most miraculous things in the whole world. I don't know how such big plants come out of such little dried-up hunks and kernels.

I'm going to plant carrots for sure. I like to pull them and eat them all crackly and crunchy. I wanted to plant corn, too, but Dad says it take up too much space. But I am going to put in a couple of bean plants and one watermelon vine. Watermelons are sneaky—you have to watch them because they creep around your garden at night.

I remember a Bible story You told about a little mustard seed that grows into a big tree. You said

Let's go plant our garden, Jesus.

if people have faith the size of that pinhead seed, they can move mountains. Not even the "Shazam!" characters on TV can move mountains. And only God can make a dead seed come to life.

I'd like to be Johnny Appleseed and run around the country planting seeds. Johnny wasn't such a "seedy" character . . . he really loved You, and that's the way he let people know.

Maybe I'll be a "Johnny Zucchini" or "Johnny Broccoli" or maybe even "Johnny Radish Seed." I'll plant. You do the rest.

Neither the one who plants or the one who waters is the important person. Only God, who makes the plant grow.
1 Corinthians 3:7

It seems kind of silly to invite You to come along to Your own house. But I like to know You're sitting right there in the pew next to me.

Look at the candles flickering. They look like they're dancing in time to the organ music.

Some of my friends at school wonder how come I go to church every Sunday. I don't really know. Maybe it's kind of a habit I've gotten into, like reading the Sunday papers or watching Walt Disney. Sunday morning just equals church. It's kind of like an equation: Sunday=church=singing=praying=a warm feeling.

If we don't set aside a certain time to think about You, our time slips away from us. I wish I could figure out what it would be like to live, as You do,

without any time. Eternity doesn't have clocks to tick or calendar pages to turn. There aren't any Sunday mornings in eternity, are there? or Mondays? or Fridays? "Always" and "forever" are words my brain can almost figure out. But then the sharp icicle-idea starts to melt and pretty soon "forever" is just a puddle in my mind.

Even if I can't understand, I still know being with You is wonderful and being with You in eternity will be even better. I want that flickery feeling to keep on dancing inside me, just like Sunday's candles.

God so loved the world that He gave His only Son, so that whoever believes in Him will not die but will have eternal life.

John 3:16

Let's go to
church, Jesus

Let's go to Grandma's and Grandpa's house, Jesus

We know where everything is at their house and if we can't find something, Grandma tells us where to look.

She always knows what we like to eat. And she never makes us eat brussels sprouts or mushrooms. We giggle when she says, "And you don't have to eat your lemon meringue pie, either." But we always do because her meringue has beady little golden "love drops."

Next to Mom and Dad and You, Jesus, Grandma and Grandpa are my favorite people.

Grandpa's never too busy to make things for me—or play games. He doesn't fake and let me win, either. He really plays to win and that makes me feel more grownup. It's even fun just to watch TV

with him. Sometimes he tickles my ribs and calls me funny names. And he always tells me how tall I'm getting.

Most fun of all is when he takes me fishing. You were a fisherman so you know how much fun it is to wait and wait and then...Presto! Bingo! You catch something. Grandpa doesn't have a boat or long nets like You and your friends used, but he can still catch the fish!

I think You like coming with us to Grandma's and Grandpa's house. You're as much at home there as we are.

I am always with you, and I will be to the end of time.

Matthew 28:20

Dad already cut out all the pieces on his big saw. All we have to do is nail them together.

After I learn how to build birdhouses, Dad says some Saturday we'll build a racing car. We'll use the wheels off the old red wagon. After that I'll surprise Mom with a planter for Mother's Day.

Carpentry is for people who like the feel of wood. I don't mean the splintery ends, I mean the smooth parts. Since Joseph was a carpenter, You must have built lots of birdhouses and maybe even chairs and tables. Did you learn all about wood chisels and stains and glues?

I wonder who will move into this house. I think the hole's a little big for wrens, so maybe we'll just get sparrows. But sparrows are all right. Didn't

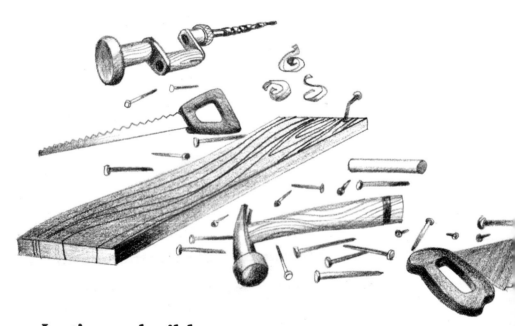

Let's go build a birdhouse, Jesus

You say God even watches over little sparrows and knows how they're doing?

There are so many kinds of birds. And some are so tiny. Our teacher says hummingbirds are so little five babies can fit into an ordinary teaspoon.

Oh, Oh. I hit my thumb again. That's what happens when I think about hummingbirds instead of hammers.

Will the birds who live in this house know that I really care about them?

God showed His love for us by sending His only Son into the world so that we could have life through Him.

1 John 4:9

It's not that I'm afraid of Dr. Meyer. It's just that when I'm in his chair and my feet are so far off the floor I get a fenced in, panicky feeling.

Then I pretend I'm in a spaceship all strapped in for take-off. Dr. Meyer turns on his drill and I start my count-down . . . ten, nine, eight, seven, ouch! He doesn't mean to hurt me, but sometimes he forgets.

Once I was so thirsty, I swallowed the water he squirted in my mouth. He told me I should spit it out because little bits of filling were floating behind my teeth.

I wonder if You went to the dentist when you were my age. Maybe You didn't eat as many sugary things as I do so You didn't get many cavities.

When Your teeth got loose, did Joseph pull them out? Or did You tie a string from Your tooth to the door?

My folks and I play the "Tooth Fairy" game. I put my tooth under my pillow and in the morning the tooth is gone but a dime—or sometimes if the "T.F." is feeling rich, a quarter—is there instead. Once I got an "I.O.U."

I'm glad my parents love me enough to play silly games with me. Because they love me they don't want me to have toothaches, either. They care about me almost as much as You do, Jesus.

The Lord will keep His loving eye on you as you come and go, now and forever.

Psalm 121:8

Let's go to the dentist's office, Jesus

Let's go to the planetarium, Jesus

The planetarium is the best place to learn about stars and galaxies. I slouch down in my seat so my head is resting against the back and it feels like I'm out under the sky at night. Next to camping out, it's my favorite way to stargaze. Of course, the domed ceiling and the star projector revolving in the center can't begin to copy the whole sky.

The Milky Way looks like somebody splattered a paint streak right across the heavens. If each star is really a sun, and if each sun has planets like our sun does, imagine how many planets there must be! More than a hundred, million, trillion, zillion I'll bet. And our old earth isn't even much of a dust speck in all that space.

I read somewhere that just by using my plain eyes I can see 6,000 stars. People who have telescopes can see many, many more. The stronger the telescopes, the more stars people keep seeing. Where does it all end?

When You were on earth and looked up into the sky at night, did You remember what it was like being anywhere but on earth?

We're so small and there is so much out there. And God made it all!

God made two great lights, the larger one to rule in the daytime and the smaller one to rule at night. He also made the stars. . . . And God saw that all this was good.

Genesis 1:16-18

Let's go
camping, Jesus

God must have known my family liked spending nights outdoors when He created acres and acres of forests.

Climbing rocks and hiking back trails makes me think I'm a real mountain climber. I curl up my trusty ropes on my belt and my tennis shoes sprout magic cleats for holding on to sides of rocks.

Just when I'm starving, I get back to our camp site and supper's waiting.

Smell that bacon frying! You must have eaten outdoors a lot. You know how good food smells outside.

When it's time to go to bed, my brother and I sleep in one tent. I guess You usually had a friend camp

overnight with You, too. Peter, maybe? Or John? They were two of your pretty good buddies, right? Well, sometimes my brother is like a good buddy and we talk and talk. Actually we whisper because voices carry like everything at night, and we don't want our folks to tell us to be quiet again.

Did You like sleeping where You could see the stars? Roofs are O.K. when it's raining, but it's lots more fun poking your head out to see the black night sky. We like sharing our tent with You.

He who made the stars and turns darkness to daylight and day into night, who draws up the waters of the sea and pours them down upon the earth, His name is the Lord.

Amos 5:8

I'm just getting the "hang" of reading notes, now. I pretend they're my secret code, and if I work at it, I can decipher what some musician wrote a long time ago and play it back. It's kind of like linking myself to history.

There weren't any pianos to play when You were growing up, but I'll bet You tried old-fashioned guitars and blowing instruments. Did You ever play one of those old-time harps?

Sometimes music sounds happy. And sometimes, if it's written in a minor key, it sounds so sad. When I pound the keys hard, I guess everybody knows something is bothering me. When I'm happy, the keys bounce and notes come out "giocoso." That means "filled with gaity"—I

Let's go play
the piano, Jesus

have a musical dictionary in the back of my piano book.

"Giocoso" might be a good way to feel, but nobody feels "giocoso" all the time. It's good to know You don't care if I'm happy or sad or just nothing at all. Some days are "allegro" and some are just plain "largo."

You weren't always "giocoso" either. Sometimes You cried. You were changeable, just like I am.

What kind of music shall we play today?

Praise Him with the sound of trumpets! Praise Him with a harp and guitar! Praise Him with drums and dancing! . . . May everything alive praise the Lord! Psalm 150:3, 4, 6

The wind is strong today. We shouldn't have any trouble flying "our" kite.

Have you noticed how the wind feels clean? It's catching my hair and blowing away all the troubles I've piled up through the day.

I suppose I should have changed my good pants before I went bike riding, but how would I know I'd hit a rock and "wipe out"? I've got a hole in my knee *and* in my pants. I don't know which hurts more.

Then I forgot my lunch money and lost a library book and ripped Connie's belt. I didn't know it would rip if I pulled on it. Connie's mom's probably mad. The librarian's mad. And my

Let's go fly a kite, Jesus

mom's mad about the hole in my good pants. I need all the wind I can get today to blow all the rotten spots off my day.

In a way, you're like the wind, Jesus. You make everything fresh again. And, in a way, I'm like the kite. I couldn't get up there without You. I depend on You to lift me up when I'm down.

I'll have to untangle my own knots and rewind my own string, but kite flying goes better knowing You're running with me. And my day goes better, too, because I know You're not mad at me. Keep Your fresh breezes blowing on me, Jesus.

See! I make all things new! Revelation 21:5

I like to dig my toes into warm sand. Listen! If I drag my feet just right, I can make loud squeaking noises.

This looks like a good place to build a sand castle. Look! Here's a pail just waiting for somebody to pack it full of wet sand. Maybe someday I'll be an architect.

Watch out! Here comes a wave. And there goes our castle. My real buildings will last longer than sand castles do. Nothing built on the beach lasts very long. Water is so strong it knocks everything down. Maybe that's why our pastor says the water in Baptism is so powerful. With what our pastor reads out of the Bible, the water knocks down sin and makes us clean and smooth again, just like this beach.

You never know what you might find on the beach. Someday I'm going to find a bottle with an important message inside. Last time I was here I found a piece of gnarly old driftwood. It looked like sculpture. I took it home and Mom put some dried flowers on it.

Here's a good place to find shells. Channeled whelks are my favorites. They twist and turn, and I pretend I am small enough to crawl deep inside the smooth pink curves where it's safe and quiet.

When I look at shells, I know Our Father is the best architect of all. Who else could have made such beautiful homes for sea creatures?

Through faith we understand that the world was made by the Word of God, that what we see was made out of what cannot be seen.

Hebrews 11:3

= **Let's go** =
     beachcombing, Jesus

Let's go hunt
for treasure, Jesus

My high school friend, Jim, has a metal detector.
He said I can use it whenever I want to.

If we're lucky, we might find some Indian head
pennies for my penny collection. Or even a new
nickel.

I've heard that the most valuable coins are the
ones that were not circulated. They're called
"mint" coins, I think. I don't think coins are at all
like people. The most valuable people are the ones
who really circulate, like my Grandma. She's
always going around helping people. The people
who want to stay in "mint" condition and not get
scratched up must be awfully lonely.

When I put my money in the collection plate at
church, I wonder where that coin goes. Who picks
it up next? Does it buy some kid who's really
hungry a peanut butter sandwich?

Hey! The buzzer on the metal detector is saying something's down here. It sounds bigger than a coin. Maybe even bigger than a bread box. What do you know, it *is* a box. It's a round metal box— the old-fashioned kind ladies used to keep their sewing in. I'll clean it up and give it to Mom. She's always making table decorations and center-pieces. She can stick something in it.

We really did find a treasure, didn't we, Jesus. I guess a treasure isn't so great all by itself. It's great because of how we use it and who it makes happy.

Each one should give as he has decided in his heart. He ought not give while wishing he could keep it or because he feels he has to give. God loves the person who gives gladly. 2 Corinthians 9:7

Let's go skating, Jesus

If I wear three pairs of socks, maybe the blister on my heel won't hurt. As soon as we can, we're going to exchange my skates for a bigger pair. My feet seem to be growing faster than the rest of me.

It looks like we have the whole pond to ourselves. Some other kids will be coming along later. We'll probably play crack the whip again. Until they come, I'm just going to listen to the ice crackle under my blades. It's so crisp and still tonight. The cold air prickles the inside of my nose. When I take big gulps of freezing air, my lungs feel like balloons all set to take off. Whee...I'm floating...

Oh, No! Here I go again. That's the third time I've

fallen tonight. Before I even know what's happening, the ice comes up to meet me—Whammo! Right on the head.

There are lots of ways to fall down. I think I've tried them all. But getting up again takes more work. You be my Pick-Me-Up, Jesus. Whenever I trip, I know You'll be there for me to lean on.

I'm going to have to pull my laces tighter so my ankles aren't so wobbly. I want to slide, not slip. I want to turn, not totter. Glide with me, Jesus.

I won't be afraid that something bad will happen, Lord, because You are with me!

Psalm 23:4

We'll use these two sticks and some green yarn left over from the sweater Mom knitted for me.

The Spanish people call these "O-Ho-Day-Dee-Os," but I think they write it "Ojo De Dios." It means "Eye of God." The center part of the crossed sticks is the "eye." We'll wrap that part first. Around. Over. Around. Over.

South American Indians hang these yarn and stick crosses to remind them to pray. The "eye" makes them remember God sees everything. You do see everything, don't You, Jesus? You see the dirt under my fingernail, and the skin under the dirt, and blood under the skin. But You have more than "x-ray vision." You have "heart vision" and "brain vision." You even know what I'm think-

ing. That might make some people nervous. Some people might not want to hang an "Ojo" on their wall to be reminded that You know everything.

But it doesn't make me nervous. I'm going to hang this on my bedroom wall when we get the sticks all wound. It will remind me that even when my eyes are closed, Yours are always open.

The two sticks are kind of like Your cross. But Your cross didn't have green yarn wrapped around in a pattern. It just had Your body. You must really love me to have died like that.

You know what You are? You're my "Ojo-Jesus."

People look at outside appearance, but the Lord looks at the heart.

1 Samuel 16:7

Let's go make a
"God's Eye," Jesus

It takes two people to play chess. Usually I play with Scott, but he can't come over today. So I'll just make the moves for both of us, Jesus.

The board's all set up. See, I've got the white square to my right. And all 16 of our pieces are sitting on the correct squares.

Dad says your first move's very important. He also says to stop and think about what will happen next before you move. Sometimes I have trouble stopping to think and I don't mean just in chess.

Yesterday we were playing whiffle ball in the front yard and it flew out into the street. I wanted to beat the other kids to the ball, so I ran out into the street without checking to see if any cars were coming first. I heard some tires squealing down at

Let's go play chess, Jesus

the other end of our block, and I realized I almost got "checkmated" for good, right there in the street.

When you were a kid, did Your mother say "stop and think" as often as mine does?

Maybe playing chess will help me think better.

In chess, the king is the most important piece of all. And You're my King. Dad says every piece in chess is important . . . even little pawns. You be my King, Jesus, and I'll be Your pawn.

Aren't five sparrows sold for two pennies? . . . Yet not a single one of them is forgotten by God. Why, even the hairs of your head all are numbered. So don't be afraid, you are worth much more than many sparrows!

Luke 12:6-7

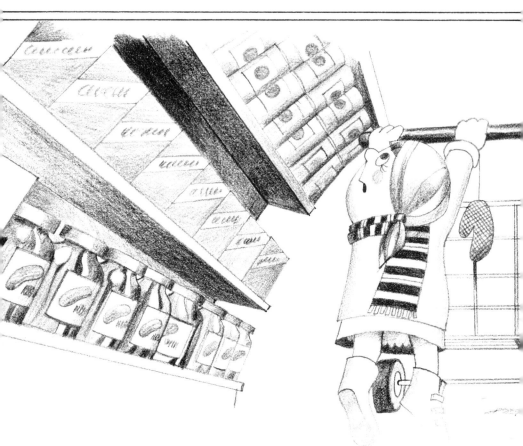

I have to pick up some things for Mother. Maybe You can help me spot the right aisle. I don't like to ask anybody to help me. Everybody seems so busy.

She said to get a can of cream of mushroom soup. Now, look at how many kinds of soup there are here. How will I ever find the right kind. It's hard to imagine anybody starving with all this soup around.

Have You noticed how everybody looks like they know what they're doing? They know right where to go and just how high to reach. I wish I could look like that. Sometimes I feel so mixed up about so many things.

Let's go to the
supermarket, Jesus

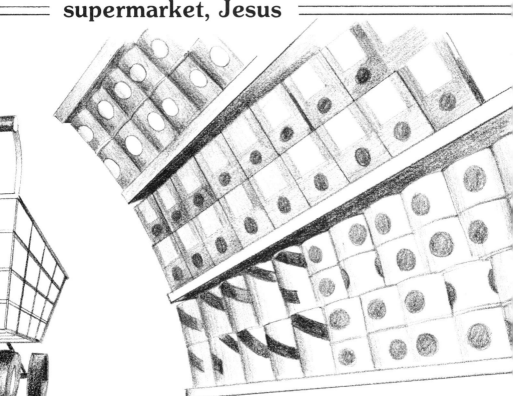

Maybe You could help me to have more confidence, Jesus. Give me a starchy feeling that says, "Get in there. Don't be afraid to try." I don't bluster around very well. But then I remember You said, "Blessed are the meek." That makes me feel better.

What if I don't have enough money? The checkout person is always in such a hurry I won't even have time to think when I get up there. Help me add this up quick! 45 and 33 and 27 and 83 . . . It would help if I had a computer for a brain. Ah, 18, carry the one, $1.88? Whew! I've got $2.00 with me. Come on, let's get home.

Blessed are the meek, because they will finally win the whole world.

Matthew 5:5

Let's go feed
my fish, Jesus

They must be hungry.

My little brother named them "Fred" and "Wilma" after we brought them home from the dime store in a plastic bag. He said he saw them kissing so he knew one was a boy and the other was a girl.

Fred's bigger. And golder. Wilma might even have babies if we wait long enough.

I know goldfish can die pretty easily if they aren't taken care of. Once my mom killed a goldfish by accidentally dumping in too many liver pellets. I guess the poor fish gluttoned itself to death.

I think Fred and Wilma are smarter than that. I hope they live to be old, grey goldfish. It makes me feel good to know I can take care of them.

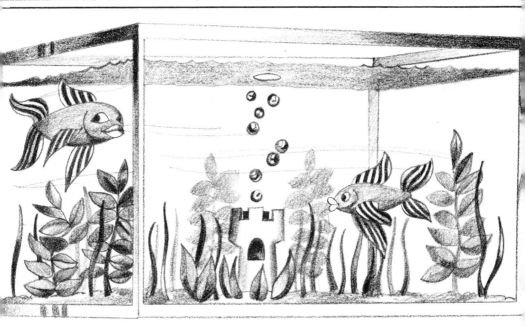

They really need me. I keep the water clean and their pump working. And I watch so nobody accidentally dumps them and splatters them on the floor.

Maybe the world is a giant aquarium and we're all little fish. You give us everything we need to live . . . fresh oxygen, clean water, enough food. Help us to be smart "fish," smart enough to know our aquarium doesn't run on its own, smart enough not to be greedy, smart enough to know who is really in charge and who is taking care of us.

If you who are sinful know how to give good gifts to your children, . . . then certainly the heavenly Father will give the Holy Spirit to those who ask him!

Luke 11:13

Bison. Bear. Bongos. Tapir. Turtles. Tigers. Our Father gave us so many different kinds of animals, we could never get bored. Capybaras and crowned cranes. Emus and kudus with spiral unicorn horns. I like them all.

Last time I went to the zoo the great horned rhinoceros was sick. I read in the newspaper it died a while later. Most of the animals in the zoo look so healthy. It's hard to think about them getting sick and dying. Do You think I should be a zoo veterinarian and take care of them when I get older?

God takes care of animals. He must have been

Let's go to

the zoo, Jesus

watching over that poor wrinkled rhino. But even You had to die, didn't You, Jesus?

Look! Did You see that sign in the shape of a long-horned skull with the words "vanishing animal"? That means there aren't too many left in the world. Alligators, orangutans, anteaters, tapirs, cheetahs and even grizzly bears are on the endangered species list. I don't know why people want to kill animals unless they need the meat to live. We've go a lot to learn about taking care of our planet.

A good person takes care of his animals, but wicked people are cruel to theirs. Proverbs 12:10

Let's go see if my caterpillar has hatched, Jesus

I watched him gulp milkweed leaves until he looked as if he would split. And that's just what he did. He hung upside down, like a fat, lumpy "J," and his skin split. Underneath was a little bag all wet and green. I check him, hanging upside down there on the cover of the peanut butter jar, every day.

You know what I named him? Clark Kent Caterpillar. He's pretending the jar is his phone booth, and any minute now, he'll unzip his chrysalis and put on his "super monarch" flying suit.

Look! There he is, already out of his plastic wrapper. He's trying to wiggle his bright orange wings, but they're all pleated up like a Japanese fan. Super monarch! Able to leap tall buildings at

a single bound. I think he's got stained-glass window wings.

We have a long banner in our church with a big butterfly on it made from colored felt. I used to wonder how come the banner didn't have a grasshopper or a cricket or a bumble bee on it. Now I think I know. Super monarch's empty bag is a little like Your empty tomb on Easter. He's my super-Easter monarch. I'm going to let him out of the jar now. His pretty tissue-paper wings will carry him all the way to Mexico. He's my monarch-miracle.

I am the One who raises the dead and gives them life. Whoever believes in Me will live even if he dies. And whoever is living and believes in Me will never die.

John 11:25

Your name wasn't specifically on my invitation, but You're welcome to come as my guest. Maybe we'll pray, "Come Lord Jesus, be our Guest," before we eat the cake and ice cream, and then You'll know You're really invited.

It's fun to pick out a friend's present. Tim likes stamps almost as much as I do, so I bought him two sets I don't even have. One is called "Famous Art," and the other one is "Fish." I hope he likes them.

For his party last year, Tim's dad took us horseback riding. We cooked out afterwards. I wonder what his family is planning this year.

Planning parties is almost as much fun as having them. Tim's stomach is doing flip-flops right now just thinking about all the fun he's going to have.

I like to look forward to things. It's fun to make countdowns to tell me how many days I have to wait before something good will happen.

My Sunday school teacher says Advent is a countdown to Christmas. Christmas is your birthday party, isn't it, Jesus? And everybody's invited.

Look ahead, your King will be coming to you.
Zechariah 9:9

Let's go to my friend's birthday party, Jesus

We'll need You in the car to help us keep the peace. Sometimes Mom and Dad say they wonder why we even go on vacations because we don't seem to be enjoying it very much.

When we start out, we're excited and noisy, but we're not mean. But then, I guess, later on we get tired of each other and every little thing starts a fight.

Some people think You had brothers and sisters. I don't know if You ever traveled on vacations with them, but I know you used to go on trips to Jerusalem with your family. You know how jumpy your whole body gets before a vacation.

This year we might even get as far as Canada. I've never been to a foreign country before. I

Let's go on

our vacation, Jesus

wonder if it will be much different than where we live.

My folks say vacations are supposed to be times when we do things we don't ordinarily do. Well ... I guess they're right. I don't ordinarily stare at the backs of my parents' heads for hours at a time. I don't ordinarily go so long without watching TV. I don't ordinarily share such a tiny space with my (sometimes bratty) brother. And going to the bathroom doesn't usually become a whole family project.

We'll try to remember You're riding in the car with us, Jesus. And You'll be eating in restaurants with us and staying in motels with us, and camping with us. Help us all to smile more on our vacation.

The Lord stays close beside you to protect you.

Psalm 121:5

Some of my friends say they hate school. I don't usually admit it to them, but I really like school. If I couldn't go, I'd miss it and I'd miss my friends. I had the mumps and had to stay home for two weeks. I thought it would be fun to just lay around and watch TV. It was—for a couple of days. Then I started wondering how Jo and Mike and all the guys at school were getting along.

I even missed my teacher. Mom says she should be called "super teacher." There are 28 of us in the classroom (29 with You, Jesus) and she has enough time for all of us.

Our school cafeteria is a wild place. Did you used to eat at your school? Did you have a lot of fresh fruit and cheese and stuff like that? Sometimes

our cooks get mad because so much food gets thrown away. I try to help. I always eat Karl's chocolate pudding. He's allergic to chocolate. Sometimes I trade his pudding for my jello. We have pizza about once a week. On pizza day not much food gets thrown away.

In geography class we're studying the Middle East so I have a pretty good idea of where you used to live. Someday I'd like to live near a lake, too. Right now it seems like I'll be in school the rest of my life. Maybe you could help me get smarter, faster.

The Lord is good. When trouble comes, He is a strong hiding place and helper. And He knows everyone who runs to Him for help.

Nahum 1:7

Let's go to
school, Jesus

Let's go make cookies, Jesus

Now that I know "t" in the recipe means "teaspoon," not "tablespoon," Mom lets me whip up my own creations. We had to throw out my first batch. A little salt tastes good, but a whole tablespoon wrecks everything.

First, we have to get all the ingredients out on the counter. That way we won't forget anything.

Breaking two eggs can be messy if I don't get all the runny stuff into the bowl. God sure made good containers for eggs.

Now we add: one cup of regular sugar and ½ cup of brown sugar and ²/₃ cup shortening. I use oil. Next we mix it all up with two insides of the eggs. Now comes the flour. Watch out. It flies around. We need 2 and ¼ cups of it. And 1 "t" for teaspoon

of salt. And 1 "t" of baking soda—Mom says that puffs the cookies up. And 2 "t" of vanilla.

Then comes the best part: nuts and chocolate chips. And the baker gets to snitch! Don't let me forget to turn the oven on 350 degrees. Now I lump them on cookie sheets, stick the pans into the oven for 12 minutes and . . . yum! If my brother hasn't eaten too much of the dough, I get 40 cookies every time.

Thanks for giving us cookies and friends who smell them baking on Saturdays and come running.

Sing psalms, hymns, and Godly and unworldly songs with hearts full of thanks to God.

Colossians 3:6

I'm a sharpshooter now. My new camera isn't as expensive as some cameras I've seen on TV, but I can get some pretty good pictures if I really try.

The first roll of film I got back from the developers had some shaky shots. I cut off my brother's head in one picture. Then in another picture I had a big dark shadow. At first I thought maybe I'd caught a rare shot of a UFO, but then my dad told me it was my thumb.

Help me to remember to hold the camera tight against my cheek. Maybe if I take a deep breath before I click the shutter, I'll get better shots.

Hey! Look at the way the sunlight is bouncing around on this flower. Thank You for my camera,

Let's go take
some pictures, Jesus

Jesus. When I look through my view finder, I find views I don't usually see with my ordinary eyes.

Mom says photography has been called a "celebration of seeing." Some people say "seeing is believing," but our family knows seeing really is celebrating.

If I couldn't see, I'd have to depend on my fingers. or my ears. or a dog. But You've given me two precious camera-eyes with lenses and eyelid shutters and everything. And the best part is my brain doesn't have to wait a whole week in order to get the pictures developed. My camera-eyes are instant-print, and they're always supplied with free color film.

Give thanks to the Lord! Call on Him! Make His works known all over the world! Praise His name!

Isaiah 12:4

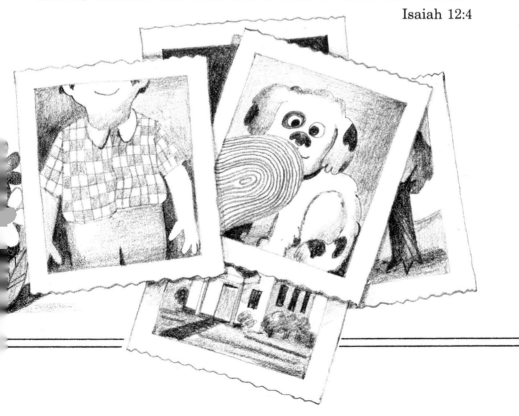

Halloween is a topsy-turvy night. It's like one big party all over town. And we get to stay up late.

Some people turn off all their lights and pretend not to be home. They must not like kids very much. I guess they don't want to be bothered.

But I know some big people who act like they are enjoying Halloween as much as we are. I want to stay young like that, even when I'm grown up.

I'm not sure what You meant when You said people should become more like children, but I think it sounds like a good idea. Maybe You meant we were supposed to play and have fun no matter how old we are.

Let's go trick or treating, Jesus

Every holiday can be your day. It doesn't have to be only Christmas and Easter. You are a part of my breathing. You are a part of my fun. You are a part of my celebrating. You don't care how I look or how crazy I act. You just want me to enjoy being topsy-turvy.

You know what? You're the "treat" that makes every day a holiday.

Let the children come to Me....The kingdom of God is made up of people like these children. I'm telling you the truth, whoever does not come to God as a little child would cannot enter His kingdom.

Mark 10: 14, 15

I know You like books. Once when You were a boy You stayed in Jerusalem just to read and talk about what You had read.

Words, all linked up in a sentence, march right off the page into my mind. Then they sit there and talk to me.

Our whole family enjoys reading. We've read *The Adventures of Huckleberry Finn* together. I think You must help authors write books, because there is so much of You that shows.

Libraries are good places to go when I don't feel like talking to anybody. Sometimes I just walk along the rows and slip my fingers across all the

Let's go to
the library, Jesus

cellophane bindings. I wonder what secrets are inside each book.

Writers must be special people You choose to give the rest of us the fun of reading. Matthew and Mark, Luke, John and Paul got to write about You. They were very lucky writers.

Help me pick out a book. When I'm done reading it, I want to snap the cover shut and say, "That's the very best book I've ever read!"

All Scripture is inspired by God and is useful for teaching, for correcting faults and errors, and for training people in right living.

2 Timothy 3:16

Bounce. Move. Bounce. Move.

My whole body gets "keyed up" to do just one thing—get the ball through the hoop. Swish! It takes concentration. When I've got my hands on that ball, You and I work together. We decide when to shoot and how to shoot.

Teamwork. You had a team, once. I don't suppose You and Your disciples ever played basketball together, but You must have had fun while You traveled around together. Sharing something you really enjoy doing with your best friends makes it twice as much fun.

When You left, You passed the ball to somebody

else. But You're still sort of the coach, and Your team is still playing.

Sometimes I think I'm kind of like this basketball. No matter what happens I usually bounce right back up again. If somebody says something that hurts me for a little while, I flatten out a little on one side. Then pretty soon I'm inflated again and as bouncy as ever.

It's good to be on Your team.

"They will be Mine," said the Lord, "My special possession."

Malachi 3:17

Let's go play basketball, Jesus